On the Other Side, Blue

On the Other Side, Blue

Collier Nogues

Four Way Books
Tribeca

for

Valerie Williamson Nogues, 1944-2006

James Carter Nogues, 1938-1993

Please direct all inquiries to:
Editorial Office
Four Way Books
POB 535, Village Station
New York, NY 10014
www.fourwaybooks.com

Library of Congress Cataloging-in-Publication Data

Nogues, Collier.
  On the Other Side, Blue / Collier Nogues.
    p. cm.
  ISBN 978-1-935536-07-9 (pbk. : alk. paper)
  I. Title.
  PS3614.0399.05 2011
  811'.6--dc22
                              2010032293

This book is manufactured in the United States of America
and printed on acid-free paper.

Four Way Books is a not-for-profit literary press. We are grateful for the assistance we receive
from individual donors, public arts agencies, and private foundations.

This publication is made possible with public funds
from the National Endowment for the Arts

and from the New York State Council on the Arts, a state agency.

Distributed by University Press of New England
One Court Street, Lebanon, NH 03766

[clmp]   We are a proud member of the Council of Literary Magazines and Presses.

Contents

The Woman Who Left

It's cold under the seats, where the life vests are.
The airline logo is imprinted on the cookie.

*

Once the rocks turn red we're in Nevada:
California never looks pained this way.
Now the salt rim around a missing
lake, a desert with no people in it.
The outskirts puff up with stucco and red tile, then the Vegas
mile in its sand wrappings.

*

Then Salt Lake in its snow wrappings.

*

Is Spokane a city? It has an international
airport. It has a revisionist historian.
A lot of clouds. New cars.

*

The announcer says,
Will the woman who left a funeral suit on the plane
please return to the gate.
It can't be me; I have no funerals to attend.
I have acres of weddings and births.

I.

Late-Stage Progression

The house was cordoned off by strings
at waist height to deflect the ghosts

who run in straight lines, their faces flat to the wind.
Once, I came out on the porch

where she was sitting and there they were,
face down in the yard in graves

like long shadows she was casting:
a man made up of pieces of policemen

stitched together, dressed in uniform
and his brother, shouldered like the golem

but whose head was very small and perfectly a cube.
The home they made in her bones

was the safe one; there they could not ruin
more than we could repair.

It was when they came through the lung wall
that she took the strings down from around the house

and let in the rest who wanted in.

Hydrangea, Best Blue Flower

Brightest against the white wood
of the bookcase.

Widow—

echo—

there is no proper name
for the daughter left without a mother.
What if I want to follow?

I whispered to her
for hours what I thought she'd like to hear,

and by the time she went
I believed myself:

there was a door, and it was painted white,
and on the other side was blue.

Kitchen Corridor

Things seem already to be settling.

Standing in front of the microwave waiting for gravy toast to finish—
tongue-and-groove, egg-and-dart, classical shapes of fit-this-to-that.
                                               I was brought casseroles

and KFC and was invited to church and said no-thank-you.
Several more obituaries. My mother's was only one of them.

On the drive back down the coast I passed (but who could stop at)
        The Retarded Children's Thrift Store,
                down the block from The Battered Women's Thrift Store,
toys and cans of Chun King in their windows.

My first thought is to kill it, the moth fluttering beneath the microwave—
        increase the ordinary speed at which I move my hands.

A satisfied sound from the cat, instead. The furies for now in a safe
        envelope.

After I Auctioned Her Teaching Materials

Tonight's essay-prompt concerned a papier-mâché jester
whose head and hands had been trimmed off

and stapled, alongside the body, to a transparency.
My mother put him up on the projector and said

"This boy has just been born to _____ and _____. What will they
          name him?"
I named him "No One Dies of Turbulence."

I wrote persuasively;
she gave me high marks.

Once a plane goes down, the cause is something else,
no matter how rough the flight was.

Blurred Farm

I began to notice that horses like to be together at the edge of a pasture,
heads over the fence or sides against it.

She might have died the first time, or the second,
and after the second
                    the times she might have died multiplied, the curve
getting closer to its asymptote, our worry finer and finer.

I was copying down the problems as neatly as I could:

the symptoms are falling and crying.
The cow is the shape of a dumpling.
                    (She began to think in terms of edible equivalents,
not being able to eat well herself.)

Fort/Da

No one says she isn't dead, the way we said *She isn't dying.*
(That's not even a road and there's a shut gate at the end of it.)

I fed her ice chips.
We were close to the mountain, and the trees were very near the sky,
      and the sky was barely light—

I learned from hospice that watermelon's also good for calming.
It's coming up on her birthday.

The ice came from a machine, the cups were made of styrofoam, the
      misplaced ones were endlessly put back where they belonged.

Mississippi

I know forgetting myself is a good thing, the best loss.
The trees look soft in the fog's distance, egg-colored light
all over them. Even the sheep,
eggy.
     The earth dries in ribs the rain has drawn on it.

Trees here grow up out of the water. Too little light
to tell what color but the ground that isn't shining is made of leaves.
So these pools are mirrors:

were it on earth as it is in heaven,
blue land of we-will-all-meet-at-the-table,

I could be for other than myself successfully
without first having to lose someone I love.

Long Weekend
for D.G.

No one loves me like your mother, now my mother's gone.
A beer an hour ought to hold me.
Pie tonight and maybe a game of Settlers, your brothers varnishing
        boat parts in the shed.

Can you cease to be an exile by ceasing to remember
the country you've been exiled from?

You and I are twins like two birds in a paperweight.
I want to push you off the bed but can't.
Last night you woke me to say

This is the order they're leaving us in.
                           You'd dreamt a lion
carrying the breast off proudly, tail in the air.

Winter White

Dusk, the deer
troll cabin yards for treats,
        their ears uneven, eaten.

Horizontally the lake shakes out
its snow. The pier light

falls through the slips,
        sleeps with trout

no one can reach.
One boat's not hauled up frozen

quiet in its curves and pitching forward
        like a good reason

to try sleeping in the ice.
Neighbors are the most-seen

least-known others.
        The privilege of privacy

—the smell of the room's corner beehive,

its promise of seeing closely
packed in wax—

I understand better when I'm less
lonely, less a fixture
holding stale bread out and apples.

How I Take Care of Her Now

She knocks on my classroom door, interrupting.
She's slimmer, and healthy, but her

skirt is falling down
so I help her pin it. The feeling is

one I've grown used to,
of stepping in to help with what

her hands won't do. But I understand
mine isn't the real dream—I'm in

her dream, and in it her skirt isn't on, it's
that kind of dream,

and fixing her dream is how I am helping.

II.

The Barn Apartment

It was a box, sheetrock
for walls and plexiglass windows to the door's left.
Also a window on the fieldward side.

It wasn't properly a barn. It leaked.
It had a sink and two cabinets, a countertop
two by two feet. Lower than was comfortable for him.

There was a ladder to the attic.
He must have built it;
he must have instructed the men who built it.

He bought the land clear, with a field and hill and creek
and a rise for the house. Room for the woodpile
before the scrub cedar started,

maples by the creekbed,
oaks behind the cedars.
He built a smokehouse and a frame next to it,

eight oak posts to skin deer on.
The smokehouse had a window which became opaque
soon after he built it.

Spiders built their webs in the sill
and he didn't clear them.
The wood of the sill should have rotted

but the webs may have kept it dry.
The walls of the smokehouse were cement-caulked rock.
The cement grayed more quickly than stone in the weather.

There were a few hard freezes
each season. He stacked the woodpile
when the scrub cedar needed clearing.

The cedar snapped
in burning and marred the hearth
but he didn't use the oak if he could help it.

When things fell apart he returned there.
The horse had died.
He parked behind the barn and closed his camper up.

Wasps built nests in it.
He built another woodpile from the scrub bordering
the far edge of the field.

He put up a deer feeder
and made a blind of the barn's attic.
The window he cut out of the wall was wide.

There was a bookcase with two shelves, a table, a bucket.
He brought magazines and gloves and a space heater,
stapled the extension cord to the ladder.

He made dinner for himself, pickled
hard-boiled eggs and peaches.
Meat went in the drawer beneath the freezer.

The bathroom was adequate.
The toilet was small and the shower had a sliding door.
The decals on the shower floor had peeled.

His bedspread had been a friend's.
The pillowcases were patterned with flowers
printed to look like counted cross-stitch flowers.

He died there.
It may have been in his sleep; he drank.
He slept some nights in jeans after wearing them

all day without a shirt.
The porch had on it his truck's bench seat,
which had been rained on.

III.

Anthurium

I need my boots and my Willie Nelson karaoke tape—
      how did this happen,

      that I'm driving to breakfast at noon with someone I just got laid by
who takes Texas more seriously than I do?

The sense I made turned out to be algebra, full of abbreviated stand-ins.

My student raised his hand and said, "But female orgasms do have a
      purpose. A female has to have one in order to get pregnant."

      You and I don't have to know what the hell we're talking about,
but we're dating, which means another month of asking if we're having fun.

               What if I say *fuck-all* every third word?

Tenderness is the first constant, antagonism the second.
      I keep forgetting my birth control, but I do remember to water

      the plant my mother gave me the last time I got dumped, the one
that blooms with stamens like little penises, she said.

She thought it would cheer me up and it did.

A.W.O.L.

The wet-newsprint feeling of someone unwelcome getting in touch
is less of a threat after three days in the car.

No glass floats remained at the gift shop, but we bought three-ounce
       bottles of star sand

                                  (the backbones of
salt-grain-sized animals) with pink corks stopping them.
       Also canvas bags printed with hibiscus in the true red of the flower.

There is a scrim of glaucoma settling over your marriage
and you're here with me, someone either snoring or having sex in the next
       room.

Just before dawn, your mouth like my cat's mouth, your legs scissoring out
       into traffic:

the door lock's fine.
Nothing is a warning sign because there is nothing coming requiring
       warning.

The Greyhound Bus Break-Up

i.

I accidentally put you on speaker using my pronounced and aquiline
    cheekbone.
By all accounts you were serious about the eggs, and Oregon, and the
    homeopathic calming drops.

ii.

The man impressed with my sign-language skills rolls up his jacket for a
    pillow, then lies in the bus aisle, napping.
I know—a fellow pays attention when you say *that's my ideal relationship.*

iii.

The whole country? The whole one, undeliverable,
stripes on the seat cover and a layer of glue left where the sticker peeled off.

iv.

You said the rocks on our hike down the Grand Canyon looked inspired
    by futurism.
The mules for rent all had apostles' names. And that woman did seem
    familiar.

Funeral Neighbors

Nightly I watch the laundromat owner
fold his parking-lot tarp into a football.

He buys my scones, I wash my clothes there.
Common professions are made more interesting

by their history of injury.
He painted racing stripes on the dryers instead of filing for divorce.

In his spare room, a set of Red Cross rubber torsos
on which to practice resuscitation,

one of which we buried Saturday.
He helped me put a tomato cage

over the spot I thought the grave should be.
It looked something like a maypole when we were done with it.

The Porch Is Open But It's Cold Out There

It's impossible to ask for an advance on the clarity of the situation:
the first funeral I went to, I thought I was lucky
to have a pair of tights bought for me.

Now my friend whose mother is dying
keeps wanting to know if I'm angry still.
                                  I do often feel betrayed by weather—

or by someone with whom I share it,
with whom I've made plans liable to be canceled—

though I can't say I believe my mother is dead
any more than I believed she would be.

Disavowal is hiding something only half of you
remembers hiding, under a pinafore your other half remembers sewing.

One tall weed waves a little in front of my window
and I think it is a person walking, over and over again all day.

In My Father's Father's Airstream Trailer

The West-Texas Nogues from whom my line derives:
> What you begin when your mother ends is a list of things you
> can't ask her.

The French Nogues, visiting:
> We have another way to say it in my country.
> We drink cognac.

Lunch is at the fold-out table in our nonalcoholic household.
The metal walls are hot,
the dog bed dented and smelling like dogs with women's names.

Over ice cream my grandfather and the Old World cousin enumerate
memorial services, then our clan's signature renewable resources:
goat milk, cabrito, the circle of corn growing over the septic tank.

I have a tourist's love of family, of being near the more articulately faithful.

My mother was grammarian, librarian, detention master, expert teacher of
> remedial fiction.
My living uncles are all pastors.

Judging One's Own Family Is Like

Carrie Williamson stole the postmistress's husband
and Pleasant Grove stared hard.

One quartz minute from the train overpass, I smell priestliness.
A string of timepieces leads from the bridge to the chainlink.
Walking back toward the bridge is my uncle,
her son.
                        "Cain't" is a word we don't use:
                             if we used it we wouldn't be speakers of English.
Her portrait as headmistress hung at the girls' business college
until the college flooded.

The small axe of love is the post office porch pointing north.
The P.O.: domesticity, privacy, buckets of feed for the horses.

My uncle breathes through the top of his head.
                             C.B., he says, you don't know what you're
missing. Unfastened, his collar comes off in the sun.
It hangs there from one hand.

The bridge speaks up: being an edifice is a lonely office.

Frozen Letter

Leaving something alone becomes a friendly gesture:
                                        the red snapper bare
on the sidewalk for two months three winters ago,
and even the cats didn't want it. It's how I met my neighbor.

We'd talk about it, his arm his, still, but in its stillness
belonging to his future,

which is to say his death from cancer.
                                Our flirtation endured

nerves numbing, a tumor pressing his shoulder the way a thumb
would press, or a pair of suspenders.

Portrait of Your Grandmother with Alzheimer's

Eternity is calculable. It has to do with restoration,
reparation. She asks her cat, what are you always
trotting away from me for?

For what? Por qué, the same as why.

For something. For a reward.

There's little time for bitterness unless you succumb to it
altogether, in which case you're lost to time.
That's one way to eternity.

Another: she returns from her 50th high school reunion
convinced she's met a lovely man. She points

to the picture of your grandfather, who's been dead two years
after they were married more than forty.

The past

won't kill itself; the present has to snap its neck,
and you are the present's emissary.

The family Thanksgiving centers around her
who no longer understands the holiday.

From the top: cracked glass, deep clouds and evergreens
swaying in so much wind.

It's not true

to say there's light behind those trees. Those trees
are all there is.

The First Year in Wilderness

i. *Spring*

My friend's little daughter was pulled
under.

What began as a single
instance of labor became
circular:

the child's mother on her hands
and knees, pushing
floor wax into tile grout
across the emptied house.

ii. *Summer*

Every window
hung with stained glass crosses

casting rainbows,
coloring

the throw rug and the wall.

Men. Silence,
great crashes of noise at long intervals.

The cat sacked out on the floor.

iii. Fall

Her prayer:

My preparations have outlasted
your stay,

so I have not only
the afterglow of you but also

little signs still
that you are bound for me.

iv. Winter

The only place open after midnight:
tall-stalked bar stools,

the valley laid into the wood
of the wall.

We stayed up
with the lottery sign's crossed fingers,

while the animals
lay down in the field.

IV.

She Leaves Me Again, Four Years Later

The hillside was blocked with
pens, horses of other colors

five or six to a pen,
and one long fenced strip

from the base of the hill up,
with dark brown horses flank to flank

not moving,
but their necks craning

over each other's backs.
They were looking

toward the dip at the hill's top,
and the stream running through it.

They were looking at
what was on the other side,

which was my mother,
whom I had just walked over the bridge.

Mirage (The Stone Rolls Back)

The sun
hits the grass,

the grass becomes
warm,

thus
the application of sun warms things.

Lambs won't go toward
the chute

but they'll follow
any goat,

who's then called Judas.

Four years since
is as a day:

when the sun ceases shining
on the shed's door

the door disappears.

The drape of cool shade
calls

across the goat-mown lawn
and I think

I can see in.

Long Weekend II

Windmills in West Texas twice, once going (the headstone not in place
yet, still a plastic marker), once coming back. In every house

she'd lived, she'd hung crystals in the kitchen window. We took
yours down. The first irises opened just hours later, in the dark

of the side yard.
                    When the news about your mother came
I thought I wouldn't know what to tell you about grieving,

though when I lie flat on a wood floor I remember how I did it.
Your cotton blanket looks like my cotton blanket except yours is electric.

God Spot

If not God,
what's in it?

The cat's asleep
in the dresser drawer.

The owl-faced
dog waits

in the neighbor's
yard, the yard's

bougainvillea arches
like a cat

over a hollow
center.

I'm near belief
out of necessity,

its fins:
our mothers' faiths

picnicked to splinters,
cast last in rows

and rows of
vitamins.

Moriah

An exercise: switch everything. Age, sex, faith for doubt.
A father and son climb the flank of the hill.

Charity Grange lies one direction, seven hundred sheep the other.
You can't ask every one of us to give our sons.

A truck plows directly across the middle of the field.
To be something that something else passes through—

I might want that for him.
I don't know if I have promised him to you. I haven't said
Here I am.

But I hear you.
Sheep on both sides now
and a tree in the shape of something out to get them.

The Steamboat *Natchez*

Cold Mississippi, topped with men my aunt might have married.
The long wood bar of bachelors stretches to the door.
                          Every man dances
like the jazz band is a great one, like his friend on drums
should have been famous.

Aunt Sue drops a cigarette into her beer glass.
The more cigarettes we get wet, the less sorry we'll be
to leave them behind.

She says we're the ones of our family
who come from stars: we two are Pleiadeans
which is why we're alone.
                          She lays our fates
at the door of sky charts and enneagrams, assigns us each
a number that predicts us. Mine

marks me as fearful,
marginally better than being driven by shame or by anger,
and familiar.
                          I believe in marriage, in
what made me, though no one disagrees
it's dumb luck a starchild came out of that.

She brooks no argument. Some selfishness is self-preservation.
I paint her nails red, the color of danger and love.

After the Avalanche

Owl pellets skirt the tarps across the barn's second story—

the wedding barn,
originally dairy but now

a wreath, a heart
over its door.

The mountain's snow basins enter April
under blue clear to the Seven Devils.

I wonder
how someone becomes a good pastor:
                                    even a small town,
a wake a week.

Death is a door, he says
or a second story
—so neat.

Also, he says, Jacob's struggle
lends strength to ours.

Whether he can feel
wings, or fur, or something meteoric
under skin—
              upside down

he turns the angel and at dawn
the angel yields.

With waves of animals
through snowless fields Jacob advances.
It's home he enters, but from the opposite pasture.

But here, faster than a man can move
ten thousand rolling pounds of snow will make a grave
and fill it.

The man becomes the angel he wrestles
without air.

He advances through the mountain
into heaven,
              or is absorbed into the mountain,
or returns as winter animals.

If each version comforts equally
are we too lax?
Who am I asking?

I hate it. I hate not having a faith.
In the barn
              the owls aren't. The wake

consists in us,

a bucket of bandannas,
everything we can think to do with them
in his memory forever.

The Party

The anteroom is darkening, the closet filling with coats.
My friend suggests it's portentous.

The first guest to arrive was her father. I've thought of him
as a handsome man until tonight

when he is breathtaking. His failures are only those she's repeated.
My friend is breathtaking, too.

I think there are two promises that will be kept. The first
is that we'll be given the opportunity to fail or surmount.

The second is that we'll have help.

I don't understand why God preferred
the sacrifice of the husbandman to that of the farmer.

I understand the farmer's anger.
My tent feels like it will blow over

or be crushed in these crowds.
My friend is dancing with her father.

Ex Nihilo

The beginning is spring.
The lanes are lined with poplars who lose their leaves to winter
but to whom nothing further wintry happens.

I design it so the marriage lasts as long as the lives,
and the children outlive their parents.

They are all startlingly easy to make happy. They recover
from unease like lightning.

When it falls apart my frustration is like a child's,
unable to say, unable to make something
happen by saying.

To speak in someone else's voice is a pleasure, but not a relief.
My tongue burns in its cavity.

My recreation of us is unforgivable
in the sense that I am the only one here to forgive it.

Conversion

The snowy parts stay visible longest.
I can see the white slope by the red light of the Ponderosa's welcome sign.

I think of it as a bargain: in return I could believe
they'd all meet me at a gate, fifty years from now—

                                           then there is what I like about
Bibles: their front page, the family tree mirroring
but so much shorter than, always,
Genesis' lists of begats.

I think about God saying please.
I am, He says. All those wives, and their names changing—
they wave. Soft where the snow pixelates them, each reddened by the
        thrill of naming.

Train Prayer

The secondary tracks
shear from the commuter line toward defunct warehouse doors:

Guaranteed Destruction of Confidential Records
stenciled above a central window blowing open.

God instituted prayer in order to lend to his creatures
the dignity of causality:

that our prayer might
cause in the real world as any of our actions might.

A while before the end, I thought
There are no horrors of the hospital at night
that I don't know.

Would that I hadn't thought it;
would that I could forgive myself for thinking it
                                        anywhere near her.

V.

Chicken-Sitting

We didn't hear what snuck in: everything is a big deal to chickens.

The desire

to bind the other to oneself,
the urge to abandon the other in the thin trees of the borrowed yard

and drive alone, safely, to a sunny spot on the far hill.

I like your problems. I like that you wear pink.

Little Chinese fans of clouds, and then vertebrae.

I liked being up with you at that hour but I didn't like why.

Supper at the Flying J

After we made sugar cookies, I wasn't sure what we should do.

I nearly bought you a depression-glass decanter.
Or, mint to peach: every inexpensive brand of schnapps and every
       flavor.

That he died in public makes it worse:
privacy folded inside out

like his black socks in the suitcase on the seat-rack.

It's like us to have imagined we could work in the car.

Every long-distance hauler in the parking lot
has a web address on its back flap,

and it's the hour
when you can see through plate glass both directions equally.

If you think you'll cry, let's not both of us, not here.

One Year and Counting

There wasn't any music playing until my phone rang and it was you.
John Cougar's "Jack and Diane" —

two American kids
rubbing each other between the shoulderblades,

the site of general fret.
My grandmother's husband died on his side of the bed

after she had gotten up already.
She said the color of his feet showed through

where the top sheet had thinned,
and that she was a kinder person for having been unable to

preserve herself or him from harm.
The times you call me while you're grocery-shopping haphazardly

are the times I most believe we'll someday see a need
to replace sheets, buy silver,

that one of us will live to grieve the other.

Cousin Charles

I don't know how he does it, even how he
walks or holds a pool cue, angry as he is.

The dead, the gone: two things overlapping,
but something hopeful slapping back with a faint hand—
$\qquad$ a memorable

prettiness of the orchard, or a blue
cloth full of cookies his wife rubber-banded at the top.

It must be possible to make decisions out of something else than fear, to
substitute for it.

His hips are like mine, the stable fulcrum as he stretches, pops his back,
lies like a soldier in her bed.

Bad September

The locks slid back, the water came level, and the salmon started running.
Down the pier we sat next to the pie store,

eating pie and wishing for a restroom.
Tangles of fishing line filled out a black shirt in the water—

not a proper scarecrow, but good for scaring.
All summer I'd thought I might be turning epileptic.

I kept smelling cat urine on the air like just before a seizure
and finally, though I couldn't tell you,

it was my maybe-never firstborn I heard across the Sound.
You took me to dinner at Jo Ann's, where if we order salmon barbecued

we'd better sit at the picnic tables, not the round ones with tablecloths.
They'll serve us beer but they're unhappy about it.

I'm unhappy about it—

salmon blood arcing over the water and the boats tied up in the slapping,
the seals squawking at each other, each holding one end of a fish.

Mother's Day

Floating with the backs of our heads touching sand, feet out to sea, how large we grow, your t-shirt ballooning, and me in her suit with the breast-
    pocket prosthesis.

The green of the Gulf scales back.
    Then your family, too, picked from you like sheaves,
so that you didn't have a kettle, and boiled water for tea in a cake pan.

Fog streams from a jet's wings and the marsh smell rises.
The waves move the sandbar back and forth a little at a time.

Her ash has some larger pieces, like coral bits; scattered over water
    these sink visibly.

    I think of how Dutch masters paint notes, white paper clutched by damp hands against velvet or fur.

Lawn chairs in the shallows, parked there, almost lap-deep;
their aluminum legs filled with water, so the sand is rocking them.

Salt in the Weather and Freshwater Draining

This evening is one part kitchen science,
one part frightened pet,

final part approaching storm, the worst
Southern California's seen in twenty years.

The other young couple is warm in the burned apartment.
We live in the building across the bike path,

in separate flats.
They're having dinner,

then we are,
then the orange sulfur lamps come on to illuminate the drippy trees.

I've been counting on how the hill rises in
small steps leveled for city maintenance,

but when I kiss you I'm afraid the storm
will be enough to shake us.

At the Viewing

Again in the same room as death, I think
flatware and barware, things on a registry someone will want to buy
because they love us.
It's true I didn't imagine this happening.

It has been hard to be happy for everyone.
I wish us luck—

the ferns will never stay alive; they drop
confetti on the carpet of my last lonesome apartment.

Your grandfather waited for us to finish telling the story before he died
and then he waited for us to tell it to everyone again,
behind us, in the casket.

Epithalamion

The addition to life of sure love
gives a surfeit of time,
in the beginning, in which to enjoy it:

a happy lack of focus
over the duration of a period of adjustment.

We have an appointment.
We are betrothed.

The promise absents a fear
which had been helpful
in its way but can now be discarded.

The full moon photographed is illogically
tiny against the memory
kept by the naked eye.
An anchor at the other end of the night,
the full moon in all its fullness is ours
only once a month
and only if we are looking up.

The promise is to look together, to spend time
looking out from what has become
less frighteningly central
for its having become double.
One self holds hands with the other.

The Afterlife Is Where My Mom Hears of My Engagement

A lot of wine at once, some goes down the wrong way.
The light's been gray this week.   I have your picture with the rose

                    whose browns seem temporary
pinned to my headboard, between framings. The last frame's glass

        I scratched in the move between blossoms
of feeling settled to this

settling which is larger, encompassing all future.
                        It's spring, many people have pointed out.
The news is fitting.

NOTES

"Late-Stage Progression": the image of ghosts running in straight lines comes from Okinawan mythology.

"Hydrangea, Best Blue Flower": the juxtaposition of "widow" and "echo" was suggested to me by Sandra Gilbert's reading of Sylvia Plath's poem "Widow," in Gilbert's book *Death's Door: Modern Dying and the Ways We Grieve: A Cultural Study*. I'm also indebted to James McMichael's insights regarding the idea of doors and their other sides.

"Kitchen Corridor": the two thrift stores are real. They are in downtown Ventura, CA.

"*Fort/Da*": *Fort* - gone, *da* – there, German. In *Beyond the Pleasure Principle,* Freud observes a child throwing a spool of thread, then retrieving it. The boy exclaims "Fort!" when he throws the toy, and "Da!" when he picks it up. Freud concludes that the boy is reenacting his mother's leaving the house followed by the joyful occasion of her returning, and theorizes that by controlling the absence/presence of a symbolic object, the child masters his lack of control over the actual absence of his mother. Freud doesn't mention in the essay that the child is his grandson, whose mother, Freud's beloved daughter Sophie, was alive at the time of the observation but had died of influenza by the time the essay was revised for publication. Jaques Derrida notes this last point in "To Speculate—on 'Freud'" from *The Post Card: From Socrates to Freud and Beyond*.

"Long Weekend": "Settlers" refers to *Settlers of Catan*, a board game.

"The Porch is Open But It's Cold Out There": *disavowal* refers to Freud's use of the term.

"Mirage (The Stone Rolls Back)": The logic of the first sentence, and the example of the sun's warmth, are Kant's, in his *Prolegomena to Any Future Metaphysics.*

"God Spot": thank you, Sarah Cohen, for the conversation on the Verano Place lawn in which you named the space that needs occupying in the absence of God's occupying it.

"The Steamboat *Natchez*": The *Natchez*, a tourist attraction offering dinner and bar cruises, is anchored in the Mississippi River alongside downtown New Orleans.

"The Party": the farmer and the husbandman are Cain and Abel, Genesis 4.3-4.6.

"Train Prayer": this theory of prayer is Blaise Pascal's, drawn from A.J. Krailsheimer's translation of *Pensées*; I am indebted to C.S. Lewis for his interpretation in the essay "The Efficacy of Prayer" published in *The Atlantic* in 1959.

ACKNOWLEDGMENTS

I am grateful to the editors of the following publications, in which some of these poems first appeared: *42opus, Barrow Street, Blackbird, Burnside Review, Jubilat, The Laurel Review, The Massachusetts Review, Nimrod, The Pinch, Pleiades, Provincetown Arts, Salamander, Third Coast,* and *Washington Square.*

Thank you to the MacDowell Colony, the Ucross Foundation, and Fishtrap, Inc., for uninterrupted time in which to work on these poems. Thank you also to the University of California at Irvine and its Humanities Center and Humanities Research Institute, the Academy of American Poets, the Lynn Garnier family, and the Squaw Valley Community of Writers for funding support. Especially, thank you to the good friends and good readers who made this work possible in the first place: Martha Rhodes, James McMichael, Michael Ryan, Don Bogen, Killarney Clary, Craig Morgan Teicher, Jack and Mary Horton, Debbie Grossman, Ruth Wikler-Luker, Ryan Cox, Shelley Ford Albarado, Zanni Schauffler, Devin Becker, Michael Barach, Abby Gambrel, Kelly Swartz, Ben Keating, Vernon Ng, Jenny Liou, Rick Sims, Justin Rigamonti, Leah Green, Sarah Cohen, Matt Harrison and everyone in Wallowa County, Oregon, and at Four Way Books. Thank you, Jeffrey Clapp.

Collier Nogues grew up in Texas and Okinawa, and has since lived in New York, Southern California, and the Pacific Northwest. She has been the recipient of fellowships and residencies from the MacDowell Colony, the Ucross Foundation, and Fishtrap, Inc., in Enterprise, Oregon. She lives in Long Beach, California, with her husband, and teaches at the University of California, Irvine, and Laguna College of Art and Design.